Advice to Gentlemen

Quotations for Civilised Chaps

Compiled by Hugh Morrison

Montpelier Publishing
London
MMXV

ISBN-13: 978-1507527634
ISBN-10: 1507527632

Published by Montpelier Publishing, London.
Printed by Amazon Createspace.

Contents

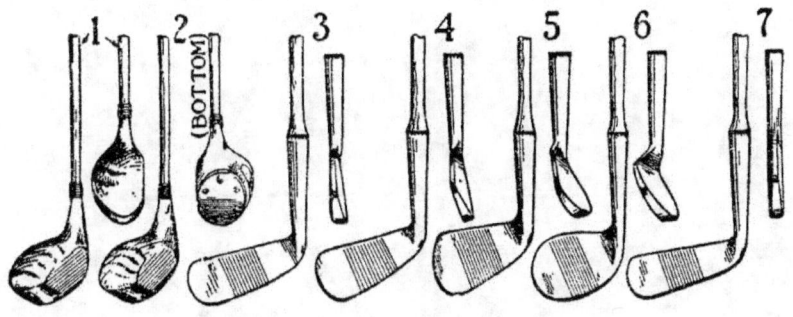

Introduction

Books with the word 'gentlemen' in the title usually fall into two categories. The first are reproductions of old books of etiquette, encouraging the reader to laugh at advice on what to do with one's cigar while holding the reins of one's horse while meeting the eldest daughter of an Earl during Cowes Week, or how to eat peas while talking to an African bishop.

The second are well meaning but ultimately doomed attempts to codify modern manners; giving advice on things like the correct form for using your smart phone during a civil partnership ceremony or how long one's stubble should be allowed to grow before it is trimmed.

This book falls into neither category. It is an attempt to distil the timeless essence of gentlemanly conduct by selecting the choicest quotes from a wide range of books on manners and etiquette dating from the seventeenth to the twentieth centuries.

I have included all those quotations which are not restricted to the social mores of the time of writing but which are still true today, or indeed would be in any age. The common-sense approach to good manners and courtesy of these writers shines through the mists of time to provide inspiration and guidance to anyone wishing to continue in the long tradition of the Gentleman.

The Editor

To the manner made: becoming a gentleman

What is a gentleman? Quite simply, as O.S. Marden puts it, he is a 'gentle man.' A gentleman is not the result of a privileged birth, wealth or social background; it is something a man becomes through conscious effort by putting the needs of others above his own and by awareness of, but never slavery to, social customs and traditions. A gentleman is not born, he is made, and most of the time, he has to make himself.

Kind hearts are more than coronets/And simple faith than Norman blood. *Tennyson*

Gentility is neither in birth, manner, nor fashion, but in the mind. A high, sense of honor, a determination never to take a mean advantage of another; an adherence to truth, delicacy, and politeness towards those with whom you may have dealings, are the essential and distinguishing characteristics of a gentleman. *Sarah Hale*

Appear only to be a gentleman, and its shadow will bring upon you contempt; be a gentleman, and its honours will remain even after you are dead. *Enquire Within*

A king is but an hereditary title. A nobleman is only one of the House of Peers. To be a knight or alderman is confessedly a vulgar thing. The king the other day made Sir Walter Scott a baronet, but not all the power of the Three Estates could make another author of *Waverley. Hazlitt*

A gentleman is just a gentle man: no more, no less; a diamond polished that was first a diamond in the rough. A gentleman is gentle, modest, courteous, slow to take offense, and never giving it. He is slow to surmise evil, as he never thinks it. He subjects his appetites, refines his tastes, subdues his feelings, controls his speech, and deems every other person as good as himself. *O.S. Marden*

Gentility was the normal state of mankind. The first man and the first woman were gentleman and lady by condition. *Sarah Hale*

The very essence of good manners is self-possession, and self-possession is another name for self-forgetfulness. Gentility is neither in birth, manner, nor fashion, but in the mind. *Manners, 1920*

A gentleman, like porcelain-ware, must be painted before he is glazed. There can be no change after it is burned in, and all that is put on afterwards will wash off. He who has lost all but retains his courage, cheerfulness, hope, virtue, and self-respect, is a true gentleman, and is rich still. *O.S. Marden*

Nor can anything be more base and inglorious, than a gentleman only by name, whose soul is ignorant and life immoral. *A Letter of Advice*

Whatever degrees you carry from school or college, whatever distinction you may acquire in your career, no title will ever mean quite so much, will ever be quite so noble, as that of gentleman. *O.S. Marden*

Good sense must, in many cases, determine good breeding; because the same thing that would be civil at one time, and to one person, may be quite otherwise at another time, and to another person: but there are some general rules of good breeding, that hold always true, and in all cases. *Lord Chesterfield*

One of the greatest investments one can make is that of attaining a gracious manner, cordiality of bearing, generosity of feeling, – the delightful art of pleasing. It is infinitely better than money capital, for all doors fly open to sunny, pleasing personalities. *O.S. Marden*

The sufferings of a shy man would fill a volume. It is a nervous seizure for which no part of his organization is to blame; he cannot reason it away, he can only crush it by enduring it: 'To bear is to conquer our fate.' Some men, finding the play not worth the candle, give up society and the world; others go on, suffer, and come out cool veterans who fear no tea-party, however overwhelming it may be. *Mrs John Sherwood*

It is sometimes objected to books upon etiquette that they cause those who consult them to act with mechanical restraint, and to show in society that they are governed by arbitrary rules, rather than by an intuitive perception of what is graceful and polite. This objection is unsound because it supposes that people who study the theory of etiquette do not also exercise their powers of observation in society, and obtain, by their intercourse with others, that freedom and ease of deportment which society alone can impart. *Enquire Within*

You may possibly ask me whether a man has it always in his power to get into the best company? And how? I say, Yes, he has, by deserving it; provided he is but in circumstances which enable him to appear upon the footing of a gentleman. Merit and good breeding will make their way everywhere. Knowledge will introduce him, and good breeding will endear him to the best companies. *Lord Chesterfield*

There cannot be a surer proof of a low origin or of an innate meanness of disposition than to be always talking and thinking of being genteel. *Hazlitt*

A man who is constrained, uneasy, and ungraceful, can spoil the happiness of a dozen people. Therefore he is bound to create an artificial manner, if a natural one does not come to him, remembering always that 'manners are shadows of virtues.' *Mrs John Sherwood*

The grand old name of 'gentleman' is now so 'soiled with all ignoble use,' that one prefers to call himself simply 'man' rather than 'gentleman.' And yet were a distinction drawn on proper grounds between gentlemen and roughs, we should all desire to belong to the former class. *E.J. Hardy*

There will always be class distinctions, for this simple reason, that ability, perseverance, and good character must make people to differ; but the name of gentleman or lady may be deserved by every individual. *E.J. Hardy*

Manners maketh the gentleman

*G*ood manners are the essence of gentlemanly conduct. Manners should not be confused with etiquette, the rules of which are constantly changing, or for precedence or 'correct form' which, although required in certain social and professional situations, are not often applicable in the modern world. Politeness and consideration, however, are never out of date. Bowing and scraping, and standing on ceremony, are also breaches of good manners.

Etiquette is all wrong and false when it makes one forget the higher laws of courtesy or hospitality. *Manners (1920)*

We must not confound etiquette with good manners, for the arbitrary rules of the former are very often absurd, and differ in various ages and countries; whereas good manners, founded as they are on common-sense, are always and everywhere the same. *E.J. Hardy*

Nothing more clearly indicates the true gentleman than a desire evinced to oblige or accommodate whenever it is possible or reasonable. *Sarah Hale*

A man of the world must, like the chameleon, be able to take every different hue; which is by no means a criminal or abject, but a necessary, complaisance, for it relates only to manners, and not to morals. *Lord Chesterfield*

The true gentleman cannot harbor those qualities which excite the antagonism of others, as revenge, hatred, malice, envy, or jealousy, for these poison the sources of spiritual life and shrivel the soul. Generosity of heart and a genial good will towards all are absolutely essential to him who would possess fine manners. *O.S. Marden*

A fine courtesy is a fortune in itself. The good-mannered can do without riches, for they have passports everywhere. *O.S. Marden*

Good breeding carries along with it a dignity that is respected by the most petulant. Ill breeding invites and authorizes the familiarity of the most timid. *Lord Chesterfield*

Vicious men have indeed been popular, but never for being so, but for their virtues annexed. *R. Lingard*

Moderation, decorum, and neatness distinguish the gentleman; he is at all times affable, diffident, and studious to please. Intelligent and polite, his behaviour is pleasant and graceful. When he enters the dwelling of an inferior, he endeavours to hide, if possible, the difference between their ranks of life; ever willing to assist those around him, he is neither unkind, haughty, nor over-bearing. In the mansions of the rich, the correctness of his mind induces him to bend to etiquette, but not to stoop to adulation. *Enquire Within*

Always have a lowly and modest opinion of your own person, quality, acquisitions, merits and endowments, both of body and mind; and be content that others should have so too. *A Letter of Advice*

All ceremonies are in themselves superficial things; yet a man of the world should know them. They are the outworks of manners and decency, which would be too often broken in upon, if it were not for that defence which keeps the enemy at a proper distance. *Enquire Within*

Some people look upon polished manners as a kind of affectation. They claim admiration for plain, solid, square, rugged characters. They might as well say that they prefer square, plain, unornamented houses made from square blocks of stone. St. Peter's is none the less strong and solid because of its elegant columns and the magnificent sweep of its arches, its carved and fretted marbles of matchless hues. *O.S. Marden*

This good breeding, you know, does not consist in low bows and formal ceremony; but in an easy, civil, and respectful behaviour. *Lord Chesterfield*

...but what reason can you have to be ashamed of being civil? ...a real well-bred man would speak to all the kings in the world, with as little concern, and as much ease, as he would speak to you. *Lord Chesterfield*

The scholar, without good breeding, is a pedant; the philosopher, a cynic; the soldier, a brute; and every man disagreeable. *Lord Chesterfield*

Manners are the outgrowth of the needs of society, and are to be studied and observed as such. *Julia Bradley*

Contempt for the social law invariably leads to misunderstanding; sometimes to more unpleasant consequences. *Eliza Lavin*

Never commit the blunder of stealing away to a side table, and there affecting to be absorbed in some volume of engravings, or finding some unlucky acquaintance in the room, fasten upon him or her for the entire evening. These are social crimes that no shyness can or should excuse. *Maud Cooke*

A single act of courtesy, performed merely because of the obligation which a gentleman always recognizes, has often made a life-long friend; a single discourteous salutation (for over-familiarity of speech always sounds discourteous, even when it is only intended to express bonhomie) has made many a refined man or woman wince. *Eliza Lavin*

The laws of good breeding do not involve the sacrifice of any principle essential to a high standard of conduct; neither does a high standard of conduct involve an aggressive course toward anyone whose ways of thinking are opposed to ours. *Eliza Lavin*

...there is an over-civility that becomes less than civil, because it forces people to act contrary to their inclinations. Well-mannered people consult the wishes of others rather than their own. *E.J. Hardy*

I can bear it no longer-this diabolical invention of gentility which kills natural kindliness and honest friendship...The table of ranks and degrees is a lie, and should be flung into the fire. *Thackeray*

Were it not for the oil of civility, how could the wheels of society continue to work? Money, talent, rank — these are keys that turn some locks; but kindness or a sympathetic manner is a master-key that can open all. *E.J. Hardy*

The manners of artificial society have this to commend them: they meditate the greatest good to the greatest number. We do not like the word 'artificial,' or to commend anything which is supposed to be the antipodes of the word 'sincere,' but it is a recipe, a doctor's prescription that we are recommending as a cure for a disease. *Mrs John Sherwood*

One of the marks of a gentleman is his complete mastery of himself under the most trying and aggravating circumstances. *Germaine Walter*

True politeness creates perfect ease and freedom; it and its essence is to treat others as you would have others treat you. Therefore, as you know how embarrassing embarrassment is to everybody else, strive not to be embarrassed. *Mrs John Sherwood*

He should not consider a knowledge of social customs beneath his notice, however studious or clever he may be, and he lays himself open to the charge of boorishness when he attempts to establish a standard contrary to that which has been found best adapted to the needs and pleasures of the majority. *Eliza Lavin*

That society is bad whose members, however tenacious they be of forms of etiquette and elaborate ceremonials, have one code of manners for those whom they deem their equals, and another for those whom they esteem to be of less importance to them by reason of age, pecuniary condition, or relative social influence. *Mrs John Sherwood*

A man should never permit himself to lose his temper in society, nor show that he has taken offence at any supposed slight: it places him in a disadvantageous position, betraying an absence of self-respect, or, at the least, of self-possession. *Sarah Hale*

It is very unbecoming to exhibit petulance or angry feeling in company. The true gentleman does not suffer his countenance to be easily ruffled. *Manners (1920)*

Hail gentleman well met: introductions

*F*irst impressions are important and a gentleman is always aware of this fact. Whilst the strict rules and formality of introductions no longer apply, some basic rules are still worth following.

...a gentleman should not offer to shake hands with a lady unless she indicates a desire to do so. *Eliza Lavin*

If a lady extends her hand to a gentleman, he does not, as of old, remove his glove, nor does he make use of the out-of-date formula, 'Excuse my glove.' *Maud C. Cooke*

It is therefore well to state it as a received rule that no gentleman should ever be introduced to a lady unless her permission has been asked, and she be given an opportunity to refuse. *Mrs John Sherwood*

Gentlemen, as a rule, shake hands upon being introduced to one another. The lady of a house usually shakes hands with all guests whom she receives in her house for the first time. Gentlemen do not, however, offer to shake hands with the hostess, leaving it to her to put the stamp of cordiality upon the ceremony of introduction, or to simply pass it with courtesy. *Maud C. Cooke*

Say, 'Yes, Miss Brown'; not merely 'Yes,' if you know the name of the one addressed. If you do not know her name, let your tone and manner indicate so fully your feeling of respect that the omission of the name will not be noted. *F.R. Smith*

The hand-clasp is a cordial expression of good will, but there are degrees of cordiality to be observed in the performance of this ceremony. Everyone knows, and shudders at, the woman who gives two, or at most, three fingers of a cold and lifeless hand for a moment into your keeping, and everyone recognizes and fears the man who swallows up and crushes the entire hand within his powerful grasp. Each extreme is to be avoided. *Maud C. Cooke*

...gentlemen always rise to shake hands. Elderly people, or invalids, are permitted to excuse themselves and keep their seats. *Maud C. Cooke*

Inferiors in social position should always wait until their superiors offer the hand, never taking the initiative in this respect. This precaution will sometimes save them the pain of a marked slight. *Maud C. Cooke*

Cultivate also, if shy and timid by nature, self esteem sufficient to imagine that you are quite the equal of those with whom you are about to meet. This resolution will enable you to say what you wish without fear of mistake, and without showing too much respect of persons. *Maud C. Cooke*

The society gentleman: entertaining and socialising

Social life in the nineteenth and early twentieth century was fraught with complex rules which now seem absurd and artificial to us. In the more relaxed modern age, social life, whether it be in the form of small informal gatherings or large public events still requires the gentleman to follow a few basic rules.

When people of good character, education and breeding meet together for mutual entertainment, on a footing of equality, they constitute good society. Nothing else does. It is only the counterfeit aristocracy, the *parvenus*, who violate the laws of both propriety and morals. *Julia Bradley*

It is a breach of etiquette when making a call to play with any ornament in the room, or to seem to be aware of anything but the company present. *Maud C. Cooke*

Be punctual. One minute too late has lost many a golden opportunity. Besides which, the want of punctuality is an affront offered to the person to whom your presence is due. *Enquire Within*

It is a breach of etiquette for the caller to open or shut a door, raise or lower a window curtain, or in any other way alter the arrangement of a room. *Maud C. Cooke*

The 'dinner at home' ought to be the centre of the whole system of dinner-giving. Your usual style of meal — that is, plenteous, comfortable, and in its perfection — should be that to which you welcome your friends, as it is that of which you partake yourself. *Thackeray*

The larger the circumference in which one moves, the less danger there is of such a one displaying or even possessing pet prejudices which are easily disturbed by opposition or criticism. *Eliza Lavin*

It is a breach of etiquette and a positive unkindness to call upon a friend who is in reduced circumstances with any parade of wealth in equipage or dress. *Maud C. Cooke*

A gentleman will never be seen in public with characters whom he could not introduce to his mother or his sister. A man when he is with a lady should be very careful, especially at roof gardens and such places in midsummer, about recognizing male acquaintances who seem to be in rather doubtful company. *Germaine Walter*

There is never any danger of being too punctual in replying to an invitation, and those who delay through fear of being deemed too eager to accept, act very foolishly. *Eliza Lavin*

It is a mistake to appear too eager to amuse one's guests; it is enough to provide means of amusement and leave the rest to their own tastes, whether the affair be grand or simple. *Eliza Lavin*

A gentleman should never take the principal place in the room, nor sit at an inconvenient distance from the lady of the house. *Sarah Hale*

People who essay dancing should thoroughly understand what they attempt. Dancing is an art, not the most intellectual, perhaps; but great intellects have been humbled by its mysteries. Competent teachers are to be found in every city, and the changes that take place from year to year are not difficult to those who maintain a general acquaintance with the evolution of the amusement. *Eliza Lavin*

Nothing looks more ill-bred than to see a young man, under his parents' roof, devoting himself during a whole evening to one young woman and ignoring the others. *Manners (1920)*

A lady who attends a ball escorted by a gentleman may consider that she has the first claim upon his attentions. *Eliza Lavin*

People who have partaken of another's salt are morally bound to respect its savor. *Eliza Lavin*

It would be a decided breach of etiquette to appear in ordinary attire at a ball to which you had received an invitation to come in character dress. Unless agreeable to you to assume such a costume as the invitation suggests, you should absent yourself from the scene of gayety. *Eliza Lavin*

It is only those persons and families whose position is not a secure one that are afraid to be seen outside their own social circle. *Manners (1920)*

If he accepts an invitation, let him take heed that he is punctual according to its requirements; and having availed himself of the hospitality, let him remember that the first step toward repaying it may be taken by seeming to enjoy it. *Eliza Lavin*

It is rude and ill-bred to criticise at a boarding house or hotel table, the food that is served. The fact that it is paid for makes it none the less an evidence of bad manners. People who are not satisfied where they are boarding should leave; they have no right to make others uncomfortable by their lack of good-breeding. *Manners (1920)*

...once beneath the roof of his hostess he should conform as far as possible to the plans she has made for the general entertainment of her guests. Confidence in his ability and inclination to do this is expressed by sending him an invitation, and to stand aloof or affect to find the occasion wearisome is folly — indeed, it is worse, and only a churl or a fop would wish to do so. *Eliza Lavin*

Queen Victoria forgave certain breaches of etiquette made in ignorance, and left her guest to discover the mistake at another time. It is a reprehensible host indeed who does otherwise, and so makes a guest uncomfortable. *Manners (1920)*

Boisterousness, indifference to those who are older, a disregard for the feelings of any who may be less self-contained because less at home amid gayety, are indications of vulgarity *Eliza Lavin*

The bachelor who entertains is a most popular member of society. It does not cost a fortune to return in some manner the civilities once received, and every man, even if his income be limited, can once in a while entertain, even if it be on a very small scale and in a very modest way. *Germaine Walter*

A young man is 'bad society' who is indifferent to those older than himself, who neglects to acknowledge invitations, who sits while a lady stands, who goes to a ball and does not speak to his host, who is selfish, who is notoriously immoral and careless of his good name, and who throws discredit on his father and mother by showing his ill-breeding. No matter how rich, how externally agreeable to those whom he may wish to court, no matter how much varnish of outward manner such a man may possess, he is 'bad society.' *Mrs John Sherwood*

To a man who frequently entertains, and at a particular restaurant, an occasional tip to the head waiter would be of service. *Germaine Walter*

...gentlemen of fine breeding, seated near those whose social development has not passed the novitiate stage, will assist their entertainers by every means possible in establishing an easy basis of conversation; and very circumscribed must be the mental range of one who cannot thus be led beyond merely selfish personal and family matters to higher and more agreeable forms of thought and expression. *Eliza Lavin*

Never exhibit your accomplishments, unless 'by special request,' in the public parlors of hotels, or saloons of ships, or other places of general gathering. The persons who sing and play the piano and make themselves bores are as reprehensible as the window opening and shutting fiends, the fidgety travellers, the loud-voiced and constant complaining, all of whom are most obnoxious. *Germaine Walter*

Men scarcely ever ask to be introduced to each other, but if a lady, through some desire of her own, wishes to present them, she should never be met by indifference on their part. Men have a right to be exclusive as to their acquaintances, of course; but at a lady's table, or in her parlor, they should never openly show distaste for each other's society before her. *Mrs John Sherwood*

There is no form for refusing wine, if it is against your scruples to drink it. Do not thus force your personal prejudices on your host by making any demonstration, such as putting your finger over the glass or shaking your head at the butler. Let him fill your glasses, but do not drink the contents. *Germaine Walter*

A gentleman is never invited without his wife, nor a lady without her husband, unless great intimacy exists between the parties, and the sudden need of another guest makes the request imperative. *Mrs John Sherwood*

The napkin is an embarrassing article to many men. Its place is on the lap and not tucked into the shirt bosom or festooned around the neck. When one arises from the table, the napkin is thrown carelessly on it, unfolded. *Germaine Walter*

It is still considered proper for the man of the house to know how to carve. *Mrs John Sherwood*

The caution to keep one's hands above the cloth and one's elbows out of reach of others, also falls under the head of kindergarten classification. The ridiculous idea prevailing that one must not eat until others are served has passed away with many old-time fallacies. One commences to eat as soon as served. You need not proceed very actively, but you can take up your fork or spoon, as the case may be, and make at least a feint at it. *Germaine Walter*

Gentlemen of the road: travel and transport

The hustle and bustle of modern transportation and travel can be a trying test for any gentleman's manners. Yet with a little effort, the journey can be made more pleasant for everyone with a few common-sense rules. The rules below for riding apply as much to cars and bicycles as they do for horses.

Courtesy, especially to women, is the one thing expected from every gentleman who travels *Germaine Walter*

Carrying a stick or umbrella under the arm with the ferule protruding at the back and threatening the eyes of those who walk behind, is always a reprehensible practice, and one that is fraught with danger, and it is perhaps more than ever dangerous when the proprietor is ascending or descending the steps of an omnibus. *C.E. Humphry*

On the street, in street-cars, and in all public places, if your voice or conduct attracts attention you will be considered 'loud,' 'common,' vulgar. *F.R. Smith*

In a crowded car, ferryboat, or stage, it is yet a mooted question as to whether or not a man should give up his seat to a woman. In theory he should, but there are circumstances under which he may be pardoned. To a refined or delicate lady, to an old or an enfeebled woman, or one burdened with bundles or with a baby in the arms, the answer to this should be a decided affirmative. *Germaine Walter*

The chewing of gum in a street-car, in church, or in any other place outside of your own private room stamps you at once as 'common.' *F. R. Smith*

The humble omnibus may be thought by some readers too democratic a kind of conveyance to be considered in a book on Manners. Not at all! If he can behave like a gentleman in a carriage, he is almost certain to do so in an omnibus, and vice versa. *C.E. Humphry*

The well-bred man or woman, to whom the best social customs of his or her country are second nature, is not likely to commit a social error abroad, because to such an one the advice to do in Rome as Romans do has a valuable meaning that is not apparent to those to whom politeness is a mere matter of form. *Eliza Lavin*

In walking with a lady on the street, give her the inner side of the walk, unless the outside is the safer part, in which case she is entitled to it. Your arm should not be given to any lady except your wife or a near relative, or a very old lady, during the day, unless her comfort or safety require it. At night the arm should always be offered; also in ascending the steps of a public building. A gentleman should accommodate his walk to that of a lady, or an elderly or delicate person. *Maud C. Cooke*

Whoever is in a hurry shows that the thing he is about is too big for him. Haste and hurry are very different things. *Lord Chesterfield*

Don't try to carry your bike downstairs under your arm. Put it on your shoulder, or you will come to distress. *Maud C. Cooke*

An idea that a man has the privilege of addressing any woman on a bicycle is most erroneous. You would not offer such an impertinence to an equestrienne, and you must remember that a 'wheel' is only a metal horse. *Germaine Walter*

No gentleman will smoke while walking, riding or driving with a lady, or while speaking to her in the street. *Maud C. Cooke*

Anything that savors of being done for effect is out of place on the road. Both ladies and gentlemen should remember that any exhibition of temper toward their horses is not only opposed to the perfect control it is desirable to acquire, but also especially reprehensible because of the air of trying to 'show off,' as it is commonly called, which it suggests and which is so contrary to good manners. *Eliza Lavin*

Coolness and absolute confidence are the requisite virtues of good driving. *Germaine Walter*

When a lady with whom a gentleman is walking wishes to enter a store, he should open the door, permit her to pass in first, if practicable, follow her, and close the door. He should always ring door bells or rap at a door for her. A gentleman should never pass in front of a lady, unless absolutely necessary, and should then apologize for so doing. *Maud C. Cooke*

Never appear in public on horseback unless you have mastered the inelegancies attending a first appearance in the saddle, which you should do at a riding-school. A novice makes an exhibition of himself, and brings ridicule on his friends. *Maud C. Cooke.*

Don't go out on a bicycle wearing a tail coat unless you enjoy making a ridiculous show of yourself. *Maud C. Cooke*

Gentlemen of fashion: clothes and grooming

*P*rhaps *nothing has changed more in the world of the gentleman over the years than his clothing. Our gentlemanly ancestors, even those of limited means, were subject to strict rules about what to wear and when; clothing was far more formal and often much more uncomfortable than the clothes of today. However, as Mark Twain pointed out, 'clothes make the man. Naked people have little or no influence on society.' This is as true today as it was in 1915 or 1815; and he who seeks to be a gentleman will be aware that, for good or ill, what he wears and how he wears it will have an impact on those around him. As with other gentlemanly manners, too much attention to clothing is as bad as too little.*

It is absolutely true, though in a very limited sense, that the tailor makes the man. *C.E. Humphry*

Dress well, but not superfluously; be neither like a sloven, nor like a stuffed model. *Enquire Within*

By emphasizing the importance of dress I do not mean that you should be like Beau Brummel, the English fop, who spent four thousand dollars a year at his tailor's alone, and who used to take hours to tie his cravat. An undue love of dress is worse than a total disregard of it, and they love dress too much who 'go in debt' for it, who make it their chief object in life, to the neglect of their most sacred duty to themselves and others, or who, like Beau Brummel, devote most of their waking hours to its study. But I do claim, in view of its effect on ourselves and on those with whom we come in contact, that it is a duty, as well as the truest economy, to dress as well and becomingly as our position requires and our means will allow. *O. S. Marden*

I have done with fine clothes; but I will have my plain clothes fit me, and made like other people's. *Lord Chesterfield*

Very young men wear their hair unusually long, but this fad is uncleanly. The hair should be cut at least once a month, and a glimpse of the skin of the neck should always intervene between the roots and the collar. *Germaine Walter*

Some men have a knack of ridding their clothes and themselves of the fumes of smoke in a wonderful way. Perhaps one reason for this is that the tobacco they use is of a mild sort. Perhaps the diligent use of the clothes brush is another. But there are also men round whom cling the odours of stale tobacco with a very disagreeable constancy...Even to men who smoke — and much more to those who do not — the smell of stale tobacco is revolting. *C.E. Humphry*

A gentleman takes at least one tub a day, and that, as may be inferred from the previous remarks, when he arises. *Germaine Walter*

Anything flashy or ostentatious in the dress also indicates a certain vulgarity in the wearer, which will create an unfavourable impression. *Julia Bradley*

A gentleman will have spotless collars, cuffs and handkerchiefs, irreproachable gloves, nicely blackened shoes and thoroughly brushed clothes. Hair oil must never be used; it is ill-bred. *Maud C. Cooke*

Avoid displaying excess of jewellery. Nothing looks more effeminate upon a man. *Enquire Within*

A cleanly man shaves every morning. *Germaine Walter*

Clothes of plain colors are always in good taste, and so is pure white linen. *Maud C. Cooke*

...it is an absurd mistake for anyone to think that a valet is a necessity. If you take a quarter of an hour for the care of your clothes every day, you can be just as well turned out as if you hired an expensive servant. *Germaine Walter*

Jewellery should be used very sparingly. Utility should be apparent in the articles worn...one ring is allowable, but not too large or showy. *Maud C. Cooke*

Always make a change of clothes and of shoes when you come in from a busy day and from the street. Nothing ruins clothes so much as lounging about your room in them. And last but not least, as it contains the essential of all these rules and hints, be always immaculately clean. *Germaine Walter*

I cannot see why a person should be esteemed haughty, on account of his taste for fine clothes, any more than one who discovers a fondness for birds, flowers, moths or butterflies. Imagination influences both to seek amusement in glowing colours; only the former endeavours to give them a nearer relation to himself. It appears to me that a person may love splendour without any degree of pride; which is never connected with this taste but when a person demands homage on account of the finery he exhibits. Then it ceases to be taste, and commences mere ambition. *William Shenstone*

Don't use quantities of perfumery, it is very bad taste. *Maud C. Cooke*

Remember, dirty finger nails betray the vulgar and the unkempt. A man with dirty hands is impossible. *Germaine Walter*

Men of quality never appear more amiable than when their dress is plain. Their birth, rank, title, and its appendages, are at best invidious; and as they do not need the assistance of dress, so, by their disclaiming the advantage of it, they make their superiority sit more easy. *William Shenstone*

Jewellery is vulgar. The ring for a man is a seal of either green or red stone, or of plain burnished gold with the seal or monogram engraved upon it. It must be worn on the little finger. *Germaine Walter*

...a gentleman avoids all conspicuous styles of dress, and confines himself to quiet colors and well-fitting, well-cared-for garments. *Maud C. Cooke*

And yet a man with a modest salary can dress very well on two to three hundred dollars a year, and even less. It is only the first step which costs. One must have a foundation or a slight capital with which to start. After that with a little care expenses can be easily regulated. *Germaine Walter*

...no one need blush for a shabby suit, if circumstances prevent his having a better one. You will be more respected by yourself and everyone else with an old coat on your back that has been paid for than a new one that has not. It is not the shabbiness that is unavoidable, but the slovenliness that is avoidable, that the world frowns upon. *O.S. Marden*

I would advise the purchase of two business or lounge suits a year for the first three years. In making this estimate I can hardly suppose that you are in the state of Adam, and I would advise you to wear your old suit in winter especially, and on rainy and stormy days. Your overcoat will conceal it in the street, and at the office the older the clothes the better. The pivotal points of a man are his hat, boots, and tie. Have these perfectly correct, and the rest will take care of itself. *Germaine Walter*

A gentleman never looks more thoroughly a gentleman — novelists, critics, and social scoffers to the contrary — than in evening dress. *Eliza Lavin*

When you order it, see that it is not in the extreme of fashion. The conservative garment will last a number of years. *Germaine Walter*

A well-ironed collar or a fresh glove has carried many a man through an emergency in which a wrinkle or a rip would have defeated him. *O.S. Marden*

The umbrella is an instrument of peace rather than a weapon of war, and should not be carried as 'trailed arms,' but like the stick it should be grasped a short distance below the handle, and the latter held almost upright on a very slight perpendicular. *Germaine Walter*

It is not good policy to carry the idea of plainness and uniformity to the extreme adopted by some men, of having only one suit at a time, which is worn until it is shabby in appearance then replaced by another. This is decidedly an expensive custom. Two suits bought at the same time and worn alternately, the one not in service will last a third longer than one suit. *Edwin Freedley*

I think it is a good principle to put on your old clothes at sea. Only very vulgar people dress for this occasion. *Germaine Walter*

Dress, like writing, should never appear the effect of too much study and application. *William Shenstone*

All scarves and ties should be tied by one's self. Made-up neckwear of any kind is not worn by well-groomed men. *Germaine Walter*

A rich dress adds but little to the beauty of a person. It may possibly create a deference, but that is rather an enemy to love. *William Shenstone*

Boots and shoes when not in use should be put on wooden trees to keep them in shape. As trees are rather expensive, one can use paper and stuff it inside the boot or shoe. This will not prove a bad substitute. *Germaine Walter*

I would suggest a general overhauling of clothes about once a month. At the end of each season the heavy or light garments should receive a final brushing and be stored away in a trunk, chest, or spare room with, as I have already advised, newspapers between them, and some camphor or moth destroyer as an extra precaution. Overcoats, which are in such general use, may be hung during their season of service, but should be frequently brushed and well shaken. *Germaine Walter*

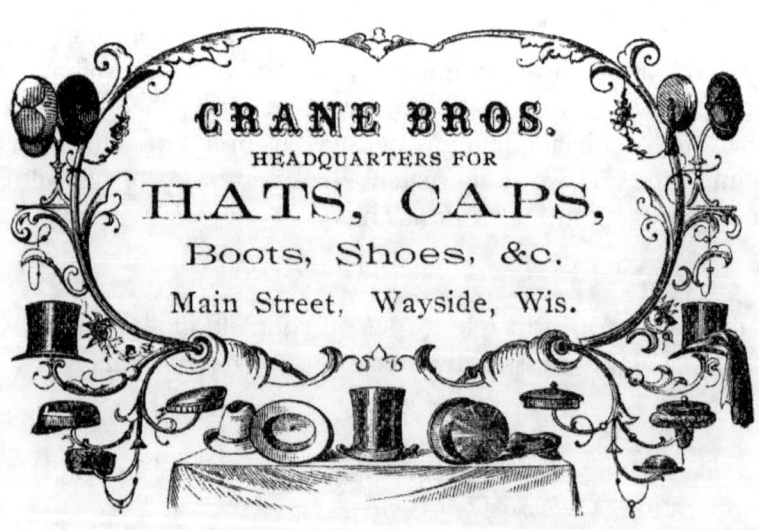

CRANE BROS.

HEADQUARTERS FOR

HATS, CAPS,

Boots, Shoes, &c.

Main Street, Wayside, Wis.

Gentlemen and players: sport

A dvice to sporting gentlemen is much the same as it ever was. The particular rules of the game are not in question: the gentleman must merely ensure that he behaves as well on the sports field as he would off it. In an era of sporting tantrums and celebrity cheats, this maxim is more pertinent than ever.

Golf: The etiquette of the spectator is embraced in the common-sense essential of being an onlooker and nothing more. Silence is golden. Advice and comment, should you profess to know anything about the game, are brazen. Be considerate; do not interfere with the comfort of the players. As at billiards, the stroke should be made in utter silence. The golf 'links' is not a place for criticism, and if you are allowed to follow the players around, you must control your feelings alike when enthusiastic or when contemptuous. Besides being a breach of good manners, remember that golf is more or less an outdoor game of whist. *Germaine Walter*

A yacht in commission is the most expensive and luxurious toy a man can have. No one but a millionaire can afford it. *Germaine Walter*

The stroke oar is the seat of honor in a boat, and a gentleman always offers it to a guest who rows. If there are ladies in a boating party, one or two of the gentlemen enter the boat first to steady it and the others remain on shore until after they have handed the ladies in and seen them seated, when they take their places. *Eliza Lavin*

Golf is the easiest game at which to cheat, but as it is a sport in the *repertoire* of a gentleman, it would seem almost an insult to hint at such a contingency. *Germaine Walter*

The proper golf costume is based on common sense. The man who rigs himself up for this or any other sport in what he considers the most approved style is either a very bad player or a novice. *Germaine Walter*

Cyclists: Don't dress immodestly or in the costume of a track sprinter. *Maud C. Cooke*

You are to be unusually careful in the manner of holding your gun, and should certainly not flourish it around or point it at any living thing, save that which it is intended to kill. Guns used as walking sticks or props to take flying leaps or other extraordinary purposes are the assinine diversions of some idiots. *Germaine Walter*

Billiards: At the club it is allowable to play the game *sans* one's coat, or in shirt sleeves. The billiard room is a place where one can be unconventional. Order, however, in a match game especially, should be strictly maintained. The severe English rule at clubs, under such circumstances, requires the man who has played his stroke 'to retire to a reasonable distance, and keep out of the line of sight'...Orders for drinks to the waiter, loud talking, criticism of the play, lighting pipes and cigars — the latter being only generally allowed in New York club billiard rooms—are all offenses against etiquette. *Germaine Walter*

The etiquette of cards calls for but a word. Whist means silence. No gentleman quarrels with a billiard marker or a golf caddie; still less should he dispute a point at cards. *Germaine Walter*

Spoken like a gentleman: making conversation

*P*rhaps nothing reveals the natural gentleman more than the way *he speaks. This does not mean speaking in an affected or 'posh' voice, eschewing a regional accent or talking only of refined topics. It means speaking in a way that puts everyone in the company at ease and which promotes interesting and entertaining conversation.*

No amount of natural ability or education or good clothes, no amount of money, will make you appear well if you use poor English. *O.S. Marden*

Religious topics should be avoided in conversation, except where all are prepared to concur in a respectful treatment of the subject. *C.E. Humphry*

Interesting talk is as much a necessity to a successful dinner as excellent edibles, but this the entertainers cannot supply, unaided, and whoever accepts a dinner invitation virtually signs a social bond to make the most of himself or herself for the evening. *Eliza Lavin*

Never tell any man you have a secret, but dare not tell it; you should either go further, or not have gone so far. *R. Lingard*

Reservedness, by some, is accounted an art and a virtue, but I think it is a fault, and the symptom of a sullen or stupid nature, and I know it to be unwelcome to all societies: I like a plain communicative man, he is useful and acceptable to the world; and be assured, that a dark close reserved man shall never have friends. *R. Lingard*

Avoid slang, especially that of the music halls or the comic newspapers. You can well afford not to be 'up to date.' *Germaine Walter*

Tell no news to one that pretends to be a statesman, and ask none from him; not the first, for he will seem to know it before, or be angry his intelligence was not quicker; not the last, for he thinks secrecy becomes him, and he loves not to be an author. *R. Lingard*

Company is a republic too jealous of its liberties to suffer a dictator even for a quarter of an hour. *Lord Chesterfield*

Thus there are some who ape the lisping of the fine lady, the drawling of the fine gentleman, and others who all their life delight in and catch the uncouth dialect, the manners and expressions of clowns and hoydens. The last are governed by an instinct of the disagreeable, by an appetite and headlong rage for violating decorum and hurting other people's feelings, their own being excited and enlivened by the shock. *Hazlitt*

When you come into company, be not forward to show your proficiency, nor impose your academical discourses, nor glitter affectedly in terms of art, which is a vanity indecent to young men that have confidence. *R. Lingard*

A man will be forgiven even great errors in a foreign language, but in his own even the least slips are justly laid hold of and ridiculed. *Lord Chesterfield*

Anything that suggests curiosity vulgarizes conversation as much as do remarks upon the cost of our clothes, our houses or any of our possessions. *Eliza Lavin*

The characteristic of a well-bred man is, to converse with his inferiors without insolence, and with his superiors with respect and with ease. *Lord Chesterfield*

Profanity is the last and most inexcusable sin committed against good manners and propriety. The man who will deliberately use profane language in the drawing-room, or before women and children, or aged men, should be considered without the pale of good society. *Maud C. Cooke*

Never seem wiser, nor more learned, than the people you are with. Wear your learning like your watch, in a private pocket: and do not pull it out and strike it, merely to show that you have one. *Lord Chesterfield*

Nothing is more tiresome than listening to a twice-told tale, though the height of good breeding is to smile over its tediousness...One way to avoid inflicting this martyrdom is to ask beforehand if anyone present has heard such and such a story. *Maud C. Cooke*

People of a low, obscure education, cannot stand the rays of greatness; they are frightened out of their wits when kings and great men speak to them; they are awkward, ashamed, and do not know what nor how to answer: whereas *les honnetes gens* are not dazzled by superior rank: they know and pay all the respect that is due to it; but they do it without being disconcerted; and can converse just as easily with a king as with any one of his subjects. *Lord Chesterfield*

People who attract each other by the similarity of their pursuits and opinions usually have plenty of topics in common for conversation, and not infrequently they discuss their pet plans and projects in a manner that is wearisome to others, who feel obliged by politeness to accord them a hearing, or are forced to observe silence by the persistency with which they intrude their special hobby upon the general ear. *Eliza Lavin*

Never be guilty of abrupt contradictions. If you differ decidedly from some given opinion, soften the expression of your difference by such modifications as, 'I hardly think so,' or, 'My idea is rather different,' or, 'I beg to differ.' This is much more polite and less likely to arouse antagonistic feelings. *Maud C. Cooke*

Good listeners should not be made to pay too high a price for their reputations. *Eliza Lavin*

The more you know, the modester you should be: and (by the by) that modesty is the surest way of gratifying your vanity. Even where you are sure, seem rather doubtful: represent, but do not pronounce; and if you would convince others, seem open to conviction yourself. *Lord Chesterfield*

Let your voice be low and pleasantly modulated and your enunciation clear, distinct and musical. All these things are marks of good breeding, and, if not yours by birthright, may be acquired by patience and perseverance. *Maud C. Cooke*

In addressing any official it is wise to remember that too frequent repetitions of a title suggest limited opportunities for its use. *Eliza Lavin*

Never permit yourself to correct other people in matter or manner, unless it should be absolutely necessary to protect someone else. *Maud C. Cooke*

Very witty people are apt to cultivate a sharp-edged variety of wit, which is too exhilarating to be altogether pleasant. It is not good policy to say every clever thing one thinks of; and anything which gains its point by making another appear ridiculous or humiliated, should never be said at all. *Eliza Lavin*

Do not, in speaking, too frequently mention your hearer by name. To do so implies either great familiarity on your part, or social inferiority on theirs. In this latter case it savors strongly of patronage. *Maud C. Cooke*

Cheerfulness is a most valuable, indeed, an almost indispensable, attribute of a captivating, enjoyable conversationalist. One's charities may lead into the midst of suffering, but they do not justify one in chilling the sensibilities of those who have gathered for relaxation or social enjoyment by recounting the experience thus gained. *Eliza Lavin*

Wit, however, is too often but another name for sarcasm and ridicule, that, like a barbed arrow, rankles long in the soul of its victim. True humor, it should be remembered, is neither scathing nor insolent; it is simply that bright repartee that someone aptly calls the 'spice of conversation.' Hence it would be well to smother the temptation to be witty at the expense of another, and crush back the brilliant but cutting retort meant only to wound, not to amuse. *Maud C. Cooke*

...it is the office, and not the incumbent, to which obeisance is offered. *Eliza Lavin*

Since, however, according to Cicero, 'Silence is one of the greatest arts of conversation,' there may be added, with equal wisdom, to the above counsel, 'Listen often and well.' Be not an impatient listener, nor yet an impassive one, but pay the compliment of attention and interest to the subject in hand, and your company will be sought as an acquisition. *Maud C. Cooke*

The faculty of asking questions without seeming to catechise the person addressed is a happy one, and yet so simple that it is strange its value should ever be emphasized by its absence. *Eliza Lavin*

Though bores find their pleasure in speaking ill or well of themselves, it is the characteristic of a gentleman that he never speaks of himself at all. *Manners (1920)*

One may display learning without appearing pedantic, and be witty without endeavoring to outshine. The path of graciousness and kindliness is not hedged in by commonplaces and platitudes, nor does it compel one to walk only in the footsteps of others. *Eliza Lavin*

In social gatherings one should not argue a point when it is possible to avoid it, but when he does argue, he should do so in a gentlemanly and dispassionate manner. *Manners (1920)*

Worries and all disquieting subjects should not be mentioned outside the circle they affect, and even though one may have but just emerged from a sea of them, it is not permissible to seem otherwise than happy and content. *Eliza Lavin*

To indulge in ridicule of another, whether the subject be present or absent, is to descend below the level of gentlemanly propriety. *Manners (1920)*

Personalities are not permissible subjects for conversation, save in the most exceptional circumstances. *Eliza Lavin*

The 'gentleman friend': love and marriage

*F*eminism and the 'sexual revolution' of the 1960s utterly transformed ideas of conduct between men and women, at least in western countries. Yet marriage and courtship persist, and the modern gentleman can benefit from the behavioural sages of the past on at least a few topics.

Immediately upon having the engagement ratified, the accepted suitor gives the lady an engagement ring. This should be as handsome a present as he can afford to buy. Together with all other presents and correspondence on both sides, this ring must be returned if the engagement should be broken off. *C.E. Humphry*

As to the gentleman, it will be well for him also to watch carefully as to the disposition of the lady and her conduct in her own family. If she be attentive and respectful to her parents, kind and affectionate toward her brothers and sisters, not easily ruffled in temper and with inclination to enjoy the pleasures of home; cheerful, hopeful and charitable in disposition, then may he feel, indeed, that he has a prize before him well worth the winning. If, however, she should display a strong inclination towards affectation and flirtation; be extremely showy or else careless in her attire, frivolous in her tastes and eager for admiration, he may rightly conclude that very little home happiness is to be expected from her companionship. *Maud C. Cooke*

A man who will marry nothing less than perfection must necessarily remain unmarried. *E.J. Hardy*

The gentleman should exercise some tact in regard to his conduct toward the family of his betrothed. Marked attention should be shown toward the lady's mother. He should accommodate himself as much as possible to the wishes, habits and ways of the household, and not being, as yet, a member of the family, he should not presume to show an intrusive familiarity of conversation. *Maud C. Cooke*

No man should drag a girl into a long engagement. *C. E. Humphry*

A gentleman should usually wait for a lady to recognize him first on the street. This privilege of recognition is her prerogative. Especially is this the case if he is simply the acquaintance of a single evening's entertainment. Acquaintances of long standing, however, do not wait for such formalities, usually speaking at about the same moment. *Maud C. Cooke*

Engagements should never be announced unless the wedding day is fixed approximately. Avoid long engagements. *Germaine Walter*

The exchange of photographs between young men and women is a practice that cannot be commended...the indiscriminate habit of exchanging pictures, or even of presenting one's photograph, when the recipient of the exchange or gift is less than a cherished friend, is usually regretted. *Eliza Lavin*

A concessionary spirit is indispensable, and inheres in love. Neither should insist, but both concede, in all things; each making, not demanding sacrifices. The one who loves most will yield to oblige most. What course will make both happiest should overrule all your mutual relations. *Maud C. Cooke*

A man is not at liberty to announce his engagement until his fiancée gives him permission to do so. It is her family who have the right to know first of the existence of an engagement. *Germaine Walter*

A gentleman may address a lady by letter, or in words (both modes are open to him) but he will find a few words, spoken in a manly, direct way, far more available in pleading his cause than all the letters that ever were penned. The more care he gives his letter, the more apt it will be to appear studied, and the less likely to reach the heart of her to whom it is addressed. *Sarah Hale*

The bridegroom should, as soon as the wedding day is appointed, choose his best man and his ushers. The vogue is to ask his nearest unmarried male relative or his most intimate bachelor friend to serve in the capacity of best man. A married best man is said to be an English fad. *Germaine Walter*

...no matter what we think, it is bad form to express any feeling contrary to that which leads us to wish all brides much happiness and heartily congratulate the grooms. *Eliza Lavin*

When a bachelor marries the arrangement of the details of the ceremony and reception are left to the bride's family, and there is really very little about which to instruct him. *Germaine Walter*

Sometimes the strictly bachelor dinner is dispensed with, and in its stead a dinner is given to the entire bridal party by the family of the bride. This does away with the presumed selfishness of the 'stag' dinner, and the possible excuse for some one or more of the guests to become exhilarated — a finale, I am grieved to say, that has happened on more than one occasion. *Germaine Walter*

It is customary for a prospective bridegroom to purchase or, rather, to have a wedding outfit made. Very elaborate affairs of this kind are not in good taste, and anything which suggests the occasion is certainly vulgar. *Germaine Walter*

Husbands who are gentlemen in feeling will recognize the necessity of obeying some such maxims as the following, which also, by implication, suggest a code of manners for the wife who desires to be a lady in her home as well as abroad.

Do not jest with your wife upon a subject in which there is danger of wounding her feelings.

Do not speak of great virtues in another man's wife to remind your own of a fault.

Do not treat your wife with inattention in company, or upbraid her in the presence of a third party.

Do not entertain your wife by praising the beauty and accomplishments of other women.

If you would have a pleasant home and a cheerful wife, pass your evenings under your own roof.

Do not be stem and silent in your own house, and remarkable for sociability elsewhere. *E.J. Hardy*

He is the wisest head of a house who rules without being felt to rule. *E.J. Hardy*

Family rules, as well as national, state, corporate, financial, must be established. They are most needed, yet least practiced in marriage. Without them, all must be chaotic. Ignoring them is a great but common marital error. *Maud C. Cooke*

A lady is entitled to special attention from her escort, but she should not monopolize his time. *Eliza Lavin*

Never demand of your wife more than you are willing to give. If you desire to be received with smiles, enter the house with a cheerful mien, and you will find there are few women who are not willing to give measure for measure, and even a little more than they receive of kindly attention. For a wife will usually shine, like the moon, by reflection, and her happiness will always reflect your own. *Maud C. Cooke*

A man of honor does not, unless he be lacking in even the rudimentary knowledge of social proprieties, compromise a young woman by being her constant escort, and hers alone, for a long time without having some serious intention. *Eliza Lavin*

The man who takes off his hat as politely to his wife when he parts from her on the street as he would to his lady acquaintance of yesterday; who opens the door for her to enter; who would no more speak harshly to her than to any other lady, is very likely to retain her first affection and to add to it that sweeter, closer love that comes of knowledge and companionship. *Maud C. Cooke*

A sensible girl will not approve of costly gifts if you cannot afford them. *Germaine Walter*

The very minute the married man begins to tell of his wife's faults, the time has come to drop his acquaintance. *C.E. Humphry*

A man will always bear in mind that the greatest compliment he can pay a woman is a respectful, deferential attention to her words. *Maud C. Cooke*

There is no code of etiquette established as yet for divorce. Second marriages should be as quiet as possible. *Germaine Walter*

Gentlemen of letters: writing and correspondence

*T*he email has not abolished correct form in writing. On the contrary, with text-speak and ever worsening spelling and grammar online, it is more and more important for the gentleman to distinguish himself by attention to good writing. It is still good manners to send a handwritten letter or card on important occasions, and a well-composed business letter inspires confidence. While calling cards are less common, business cards for the modern gentleman are more popular than ever.

A small, thin card for a gentleman, not glazed, with his name in small script and his address well engraved in the corner, is in good taste. *Mrs John Sherwood*

Character is frequently judged by handwriting. Write a good, clear, legible hand, without any flourishes, and always use the best and the blackest of ink. The typewriter is employed only for business correspondence. *Germaine Walter*

A single misspelled word acts unfavorably against the writer of a letter. A missive thus defaced prejudices the stranger whom he may have occasion to address and establishes an unfavorable basis for the opinion the recipient may form of him. *Eliza Lavin*

It is hardly necessary to say that a business card should never be used as a visiting card. A gentleman carries his cards either in his pocket or in a small leather case sold for that purpose. *Maud C. Cooke*

Perhaps there is nothing which marks the lady or gentleman more than the mode in which they write a letter or note. And yet, strange as it may appear, this is a branch of education which is singularly neglected. It is surprising how many persons of refinement, cultivation, and even of some literary attainment, write in an inelegant and careless manner. *C.E. Humphry*

Letter writing is an art, and there is no pleasure equal to that of receiving and reading a chatty and well-worded epistle from some dear friend. *Germaine Walter*

In business letters be brief and to the point. *Germaine Walter*

Gentlemen's clubs

Sadly today the term 'gentlemen's club' has been degraded to describe an establishment that few gentlemen are likely to enter. Although less popular than at one time, traditional gentlemen's clubs still exist in Britain, the USA and some parts of the Commonwealth. The concept of a club is sometimes a little unfamiliar to modern gentlemen: it is not a commercial establishment run for monetary gain but a mutually owned society where the premises are considered to be an extension of the members' homes. The etiquette and rules of behaviour have changed little in most clubs over the years, and so this short chapter is included for reference for any gentlemen visiting or hoping to join a club.

If a man wishes to get on socially, he should belong to at least one good club. It gives him his standing in the community, and places him. He is no longer on the list of the unidentified. *Germaine Walter*

Club etiquette is very simple. It is only the application of the usual rules of courtesy observed in private life. The club is your home. You should behave there as you would in your own house as host, and consequently your conduct toward your fellow-members should be characterized by the utmost consideration. *Germaine Walter*

I myself have seen, at my favourite Club (the Senior United Service), His Grace the Duke of Wellington quite contented with the joint, one-and-three, and half-pint of sherry, nine; and if his Grace, why not you and I? *Thackeray*

A clubman never pays an attendant for refreshment or food served. Gratuities of any kind to servants are forbidden. *Germaine Walter*

A man does not remove his coat or sit in his shirtsleeves in any of the public rooms. An allowance, however, is made in the billiard room. *Germaine Walter*

The club is not a place to conduct one's commercial interests. Invitations and special correspondence can be conducted on club paper, but certainly it is a breach of club etiquette to use it for business purposes. *Germaine Walter*

It is not club etiquette to 'treat.' You can do so if you desire, but you are not obliged to follow this inane custom, which is born of bar-room ethics. *Germaine Walter*

God is a gentleman: religious observance

In times past the true gentleman was thought to be on a par with the true Christian. In our more secular age, religion is of less importance and positively reviled by some, but the modern gentleman of any religion or none will still from time to time need to be aware of good manners and consideration for others in matters of religious observance.

It is the heart that makes both the true gentleman and the great theologian. The Apostle Paul always endeavoured to conciliate his audience when he commenced addressing them. And his letters, as well as those of his fellow-apostles, are full of sympathy and consideration for every one's feelings, because he had learned from Him whose sympathy extended to even the greatest of sinners. *E.J. Hardy*

It is always proper and courteous for a person in church to share either prayer-book or hymnal with anyone who may be without either. *Manners (1920)*

The precepts of Jesus Christ are patterns on which to form the character of a perfect gentleman. What a lesson in politeness is His rebuke of the forward manner of those who press eagerly on to get the upper seats at banquets! The apostles also left us many injunctions to gentleness and courteousness of manner, which should form the basis of every manual of good behavior. *Sarah Hale*

But when you frequent places of public worship, as I would have you go to all the different ones you meet with, remember that however erroneous, they are none of them objects of laughter and ridicule. *Lord Chesterfield*

It is, in fact, not only rude, but irreverent, to be late in church for the beginning of the service. If one should be accidentally late, it is good manners to wait till the congregation rises from the kneeling posture before making one's way to a seat. It is almost an awful thing to interrupt a prayer. But I have seen people do it with no more scruple than if they were passing in a crowded street. *C.E. Humphry*

...those who regard baptism more in the light of a beautiful symbol are in favor of making it memorable by its associations, as well as its purpose. *Eliza Lavin*

Reverence for the sacred place conduces to a quiet manner; but this is not always felt by those who attend public worship. *C.E. Humphry*

Well-bred people attend church in simple costumes, free from display. These may be of rich materials, but they are quiet in color and make. The church is not the place to flaunt elegant attire in the face of less fortunate worshipers in the 'I-am-richer-than-thou' style that marks the *parvenu. Maud C. Cooke*

Where, for instance, could a better law of good manners be found than in the Book of Books? A glance at the end of the fourth chapter of Ephesians will show a code of conduct that, if followed, would make a man a perfect member of society. *C.E. Humphry*

A reverence for religious observances is a distinguishing trait of a refined mind...a lack of reverence in the house of God implies low parentage, or a coarse nature that is not subject to refinement. *C.E. Humphry*

Pattern after Him who gave the Golden Rule, and who was the first true gentleman that ever breathed. *O.S. Marden*

The gentleman is dead: funerals and mourning

Elaborate mourning rituals were once a feature of every gentleman's life. The move to a more secular society, and the huge death toll of the First World War, gradually pushed funerals and even the subject of death itself into something approaching a taboo. A few common sense rules still apply, which the modern gentleman will find reassuringly useful in the times of loss which sadly affect us all.

While the question whether black clothing is a fitting garb for those who sorrow is one which cannot be decided by one person for another, good taste directs that at least as much attention be paid the attire of those who honor the departed friend as would be shown the living. *Eliza Lavin*

In making a call after death has visited any family, the dress of the caller should be attuned to the occasion, and should be of a sombre order, though it need not be precisely mourning. *C.E. Humphry*

With the past are buried many of the customs that intensified the gloom of which not even the most hopeful teachings of Christianity has robbed death, and many ceremonies once considered inseparable from the rites of burial are now held, and with good reason, to be in very bad taste. *Eliza Lavin*

The caller takes his tone from that of the family. It is in the worst taste to refer to the loss sustained unless the initiative is taken by one of those bereaved. *C.E Humphry*

A refined sensibility does not permit one who is not a sharer in grief to witness its demonstration, and the most thoughtful attention which friendship can pay at this moment is expressed by withdrawal. *Eliza Lavin*

By a card left in person after the decease, by a brief note of sympathy or a few flowers (which always speak kindly for us), the aching heart may know that its sorrow has been shared and respected. *Eliza Lavin*

The use of flowers at funerals is a beautiful custom, and its only disparagement is the tendency to make them the vehicle of ill-timed display or the expression of extravagant laudation or absurd symbolism, instead of allowing them to speak their own beautiful language of love and hope. Any attempt to make them up into unnatural shapes is in bad taste, though they may be grouped with special reference to their fitness for the occasion. *Eliza Lavin*

Should you send flowers, do not purchase or order any set designs. They are hideous-remind one of the tenement funerals, and are strikingly inappropriate. *Germaine Walter*

Long formal letters of condolence are never written by those sympathetic persons who have the perception to understand that such epistles serve only to turn the knife in the wound. A person cannot tell another just what to say, but to all it may be said, spare the afflicted the task of reading long exhortations or homilies, and do not indulge in recountals of similar losses (sympathy sometimes has a morbid propensity to do this); think twice before constituting yourself a mentor; do not revive griefs that are yielding to the kindly influences of time, but never refrain from writing a few words of love and sympathy to those in deep trouble. A kind thought, transcribed in words which the bereaved may keep in memory, never comes amiss and cannot come too soon. *Eliza Lavin*

However this may be, it is best not to let one's language suggest that the time for fittingly impressing a moral or religious lesson has arrived. Perhaps it has, but not to all has been given the privilege or the power to teach. Let the written words be few and as direct as may be, from the heart to the heart. *Eliza Lavin*

A gentleman's miscellany

*H*ere are a few final quotes which do not fit under the heading of any particular topic. I will leave the final summing up to the poetry of Sir Henry Wooton, whose words are as true today as they were in 1530.

For manners are not idle, but the fruit
Of loyal nature and of noble mind. *Tennyson*

Observe carefully, then, what displeases or pleases you in others, and be persuaded that in general the same things will please or displease them in you. *Lord Chesterfield*

The terms 'lady' and 'gentleman' are distinctive. Your friends and acquaintances are all supposed to be ladies and gentlemen. To distinguish them as such implies a doubt. *Germaine Walter*

Life in an hotel or boarding house tends to make people careless in manners and even selfish, but the true gentleman will not permit himself to neglect, at table or elsewhere, those forms which are the outward evidence of good breeding. *Manners (1920)*

Money is not essential... Diogenes, Socrates, and Epaminondas are gentlemen of the best blood, who have chosen the condition of poverty, when that of wealth was equally open to them. *Emerson*

The economy which is a part of every Englishman's religion could well be copied in America. Even a duchess tries to save money, saying wisely that it is better to give it away in charity than to waste it. *Mrs John Sherwood*

It is best to buy for cash. You can always buy cheaper in this way. If you make bills, however, pay them promptly. Make no bill you are not sure of paying at the time promised by you. Avoid debt as the greatest curse of life. *Maud C. Cooke*

Bravado is often the inefficient armor of bashfulness and sometimes the offensive demonstration of indifference or egotism. For whatever reason assumed, it is never creditable and often leads to most unpleasant reflections. *Eliza Lavin*

Allow yourself some time for business every day; no man should be in the world, that has nothing to do in it; yet never proclaim yourself very busy...the less busy you seem, the more you are admired when your work is dispatched. *R. Lingard*

Be upon your guard against the pedantry and affectation of business, which young people are apt to fall into from the pride of being concerned in it young. They look thoughtful, complain of the weight of business, throw out mysterious hints, and seem big with secrets which they do not know. Do you, on the contrary, never talk of business, but to those with whom you are to transact it; and learn to seem vacuous, and idle, when you have the most business. *Lord Chesterfield*

A little formality is necessary to counteract the overflow of spirits which is apt to be manifested when several children meet together... No one would rob children of the right to frolic, but a wise discrimination should be made as to time and place. *Eliza Lavin*

Rise early, and at the same hour every morning, how late soever you may have sat up the night before. This secures you an hour or two, at least, of reading or reflection, before the common interruptions of the morning begin; and it will save your constitution, by forcing you to go to bed early, at least one night in three. *Lord Chesterfield*

Show your appreciation cordially, but avoid excessive applause. Never stamp your feet or whistle. Carried beyond a certain point, applause ceases to be a courtesy. *F.R. Smith*

There is something infinitely better than to be a millionaire of money, and that is to be a millionaire of brains, of culture, of helpfulness to one's fellows, a millionaire of character – a gentleman. *O.S. Marden*

A gentleman makes no noise. *Emerson*

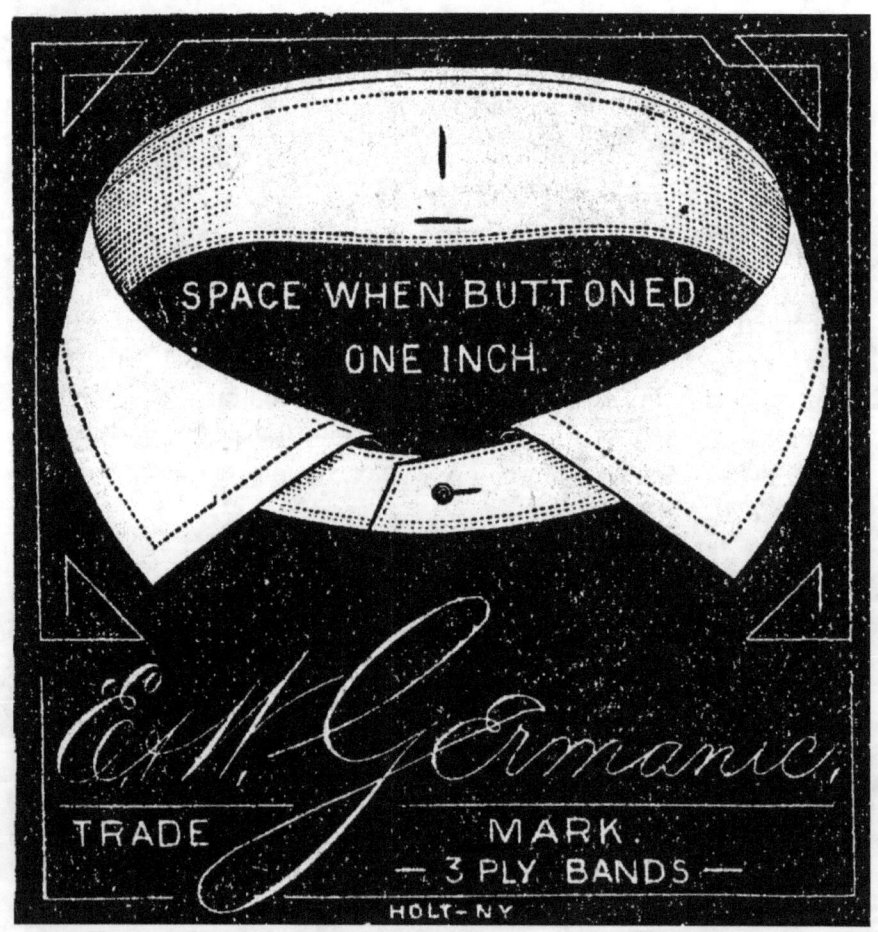

The Happy Man, or True Gentleman.

How happy is he born or taught,
That serveth not another's will,
Whose armour is his honest thought,
And simple truth his only skill:

Whose passions not his masters are.
Whose soul is still prepared for death
Not tied unto the world with care
Of prince's ear, or vulgar breath:

Who hath his life from rumours freed,
Whose conscience is his strong retreat
Whose state can neither flatterers feed.
Nor ruin make oppressors great,

Who God doth late and early pray
More of His grace than gifts to lend;
And entertains the harmless day
With a well-chosen book or friend;

This man is freed from servile bands,
Of hope to rise or fear to fall;
Lord of himself, though not of lands,
And having nothing, yet hath all.

Sir Henry Wotton, 1530.

Bibliography

Anonymous. *A letter of advice to a young gentleman of an honourable family.* R. Vlavell, London, 1688

Anonymous. *Enquire Within.* Houlston and Sons, London, 1894

Anonymous. *Manners.* McClelland and Stewart Ltd, Toronto, 1920

Bradley, Julia M. *Modern Manners and Social Forms.* James B. Smiley, Chicago, 1889

Chesterfield, Earl of. *Lord Chesterfield's Letters to His Son.* W.Scott, London, 1889 (First published 1774)

Cooke, Maud C. *Social Etiquette, or, Manners and Customs of Polite Society.* The Matthews-Northrup Co, Buffalo, N.Y. 1896

Emerson, Ralph Waldo. *Manners.* H. Altemus, Philadelphia, 1896

Freedley, Edwin T. *The Secret of Success in Life, or, common sense in business and the home.* J.S. Robertson and Bros, Whitby, Ontario, 1881

Hale, Sarah Josepha Buell. *Manners.* J.E. Tilton and Co, Boston, 1868

Hardy, Edward John. *Manners Makyth Man.* C. Scribner and Sons, New York, 1887

Hazlitt, William. *Men and Manners.* Ward, Lock and Co, London, 1852

Humphry, C.E. *Manners for Men.* James Bowden, London 1897
Lavin, Eliza M. *Good Manners.* Butterick Publishing Company Ltd, New York, 1889

Lingard, Rev. Dr. Richard. *A letter of advice to a young gentleman leaving the university, concerning his behaviour and conversation in the world.* V.V. Bradford, New York, 1696

Marden, Orrison Swett. *Pushing to the Front.* Success Company, Petersburg, New York, 1911

Shenstone, William. *Essays on Men and Manners.* Bradbury Evans and Co, London 1868

Sherwood, Mrs John M.E.W. *Manners and Social Usages.* Harper and Brothers, New York, 1887

Smith, F.R. *Manners and Conduct In School and Out.* Allyn and Bacon, Boston, 1921

Thackeray, William Makepeace. *The Book of Snobs.* Bradbury and Evans, London, 1856

Walter, Germaine. *The Complete Bachelor Manners for Men.* D. Appleton and Co, New York, 1896

If you enjoyed this book, or even if you didn't, please leave a review at Amazon. We appreciate your feedback and always strive to improve our publications.

Other books from Montpelier Publishing

Available from Amazon

The Slow Bicycle Companion

The Pipe Smoker's Companion

The Real Ale Companion

The Cigar Collection

The Men's Guide to Frugal Grooming

The Frugal Gentleman

www.ingramcontent.com/pod-product-compliance
Lightning Source LLC
Chambersburg PA
CBHW071124280526
45787CB00003B/1160